Stock Market
Knowledge
for All Ages

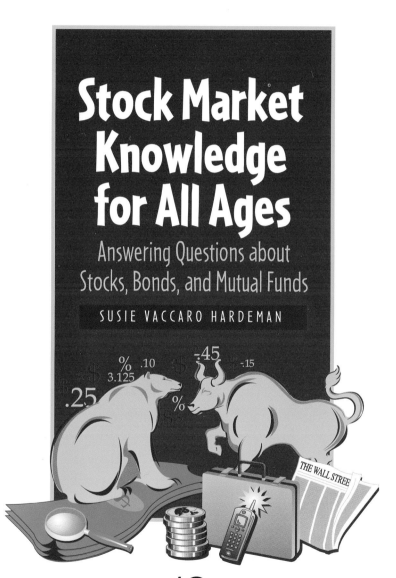

Stock Market Knowledge for All Ages

Answering Questions about
Stocks, Bonds, and Mutual Funds

SUSIE VACCARO HARDEMAN

TEN SPEED PRESS
Berkeley | Toronto

Ten Speed Press
Box 7123
Berkeley, California 94707
www.tenspeed.com

Distributed in Australia by Simon and Schuster Australia, in Canada by Ten Speed Press Canada, in New Zealand by Southern Publishers Group, in South Africa by Real Books, and in the United Kingdom and Europe by Airlift Book Company.

Cover and text design by Diana Craft
Editing by Linda Hassler

Photograph on page 63 copyright © 2004 by Chuck Fandrei

Library of Congress Cataloging-in-Publication Data is on file with the publisher.

ISBN 1-58008-627-6

Printed in Hong Kong
First printing, 2004

This book is dedicated to
Joshua Matthews,
my friend.

CONTENTS

Preface

In July 2001, my husband and I moved to Little Rock, Arkansas. Tyler was in the final stages of cancer and wanted to return home. I was on a walker due to an accident earlier in the year. It meant so much to Tyler to see his old friends before his death, which came after only three weeks in Little Rock.

The very afternoon following his memorial service I was surprised by a knock at my door. There stood a delightful, cheery thirteen-year-old young man. Joshua Matthews was selling items to raise money for his school band. He saw my two miniature poodles and, informing me that he wanted to be a veterinarian when he grew up, he asked if he could come by and walk the dogs after school. Because it was difficult for me to get around on the walker, I was thrilled and thanked him for offering.

The months went by and he never failed to appear. The dogs loved Joshua and eagerly awaited their afternoon walk. If he couldn't come, he always called. He never asked for payment of any kind. Upon meeting Joshua's mother, I told her that she had a very responsible and pleasant son.

On one of his daily visits, Joshua informed me that when he earned his first paycheck as a veterinarian, he wanted to buy Coca-Cola stock. Christmas was approaching so I called his mother and told her that I wanted to open a brokerage account for Joshua and purchase Coca-Cola stock to thank him for all he had done for me. I called a broker at a national firm to make an appointment. I also asked him to please have some brochures, pamphlets, or any other materials that would be appropriate to give to a young man who knows nothing about the stock market.

Upon our arrival, I asked the broker for the information he had gathered and he informed me that there was nothing available for students. That was all I needed to hear. The next day, I left for California for the holidays. During the two months I was there, I began interviewing my friends' children and grandchildren. My question to each one was "What do you want to know about the stock market?"

Upon my return to Little Rock, I contacted several school librarians to see if they had any books on the stock market that were for students. Repeatedly, the answer was "No!" When I revealed that I was writing such a book, they all asked to be called as soon as the book was available. Over the next few months, I began visiting schools and making presentations to groups of students. I found that teachers and administrators were thrilled to allocate a school period. Participation by the students was often voluntary, but the room was always packed. They were eager to ask questions about the stock market. A friend always accompanied me and wrote down the questions.

The following summer, these meetings were expanded to camps and other places where there were kids eager to participate. These visits were extremely gratifying and informative, to say nothing of the tremendous interest and curiosity the students had for the subject. I have been completely overwhelmed at the high caliber of the questions and the level of interest and enthusiasm expressed by these students. Having thoroughly researched the market, I have found nothing in print that is geared for their age group.

During the time I have spent researching, interviewing, and talking with hundreds of people, I also have discovered that if answers to basic questions about the stock market could be presented in a colorful and interesting way, the appeal is universal. I have had tremendous interest from young adults, men, women, professionals, and educators—people of all ages.

Without a doubt, the questions and encouragement from the students and adults have made this project come to fruition. However, if it weren't for Joshua's kindness on a day when I really needed it, this book would not have been written. His thirst for knowledge about the workings of the stock market has resulted in *Stock Market Knowledge for All Ages*. It is my sincere hope that this book serves Joshua and others well.

Acknowledgments

I am indebted to Mary Ann Holt, Lisa Lo Porto, Mary Worthen, and Mary Ruth Brown for their guidance and direction in writing this book. Their advice was invaluable, as was that of Milli Brown at Brown Books Publishing Group.

I wish to thank Mr. Warren Stephens of Stephens, Inc. in Little Rock for believing in my book as well as printing its first edition.

To Diana Craft, designer extraordinaire! Her incredible talent truly brought this book to life! What a pleasure it has been working with this gal! She has truly made this project exciting and fun.

I owe a tremendous thanks to John Peace for always finding time to accompany me to various appointments and graciously counseling me.

Special thanks to John Bumpers. Without his constant guidance through this process, this book would never have evolved. His superb business acumen led the way.

My constant thanks to John Carroll, who has been with me since the beginning and continues to be. He has always been encouraging and has guided me with his expertise in answering technical questions (he is a registered stockbroker). His friendship is one of the highlights of having written this book.

I was fortunate, thanks to Brian Randolph at Camp Cheley located in Estes Park, Colorado, to have an evening with the campers and counselors who contributed excellent questions for my book. The campers were terribly enthusiastic and very knowledgeable about the stock market. I am thankful to Don Cheley, owner of Camp Cheley, as well as Brian, for making such a memorable evening possible.

My friend, Linda Robbins, has believed in this project since its inception. As a teacher in Dana Point, California, she knew of the need for a book like mine to be available to students everywhere.

To Mrs. Eloise Hudson, principal at Forrest Heights Junior High, I say thank you for your interest in this project and your willingness to help. I will always remember your tenacity in attempting to use my book as part of your curriculum.

Lastly, thanks go to my good friend Gus Dobbs, without whom this book would not have come to fruition. Since the beginning, Gus has lent support, confidence, encouragement, and a sincere belief this could happen. He has been there daily, and I shall always be indebted to him for his friendship.

Introduction

Stock Market Knowledge for All Ages is designed to make everyone have fun while learning the workings of the various stock markets.

This publication is reader friendly and is a reference tool to help the reader become familiar with the meaning of the terms as well as offering definitions of the most widely used vocabulary.

I hope you find this book to be a refreshing and wonderful learning experience.

History of
Wall Street

HISTORY OF WALL STREET

People know investing occurs on Wall Street but the complexities scare them, and because of this, the stock market remains a mystery. The purpose of this book is to explain how stocks are bought and sold.

How did Wall Street get its name?

In 1626, the Dutch purchased the island of Manhattan for $24 and some beads. It was purchased from local Indians. The settlers built a wall from twigs and mud beside a street. This was done after establishing a trading post on the island. The Dutch named the street Wall Street.

What were the first securities to be traded?

Eighty million dollars in government bonds were issued to help pay for the war against England. These were the first national securities to be traded.

Where were the first stocks traded?

The First Bank of the United States, the first federally chartered bank, added bank stocks to the government bonds. Alexander Hamilton, the Secretary of the Treasury, offered shares of the Bank's stock to the public.

Where and when was the first stock exchange established?

The first stock exchange was established in Philadelphia in 1790. Because of there being so much interest by merchants to buy stocks and bonds, a market was established for trading.

Where did the term over-the-counter come from?

It got its name from merchants, who sold their securities over the counter quite the same way they sold their wares.

WALL STREET

What were the workings of the market?

Some of the merchants who wanted to organize a market formed a central auction at 22 Wall Street. Their securities were traded every day at noon. The securities were left with the auctioneers who received money (commission) for the stocks and bonds that were sold. An agent or broker, who represented the investor, also received a commission for the stocks and bonds purchased.

Who became the founders of the New York Stock Exchange?

The Wall Street leaders met on March 21, 1792, and established an improved market. Twenty-four New York City stockbrokers and merchants signed the Buttonwood Agreement two months later. They agreed to trade securities amongst themselves and set commission rates. These men became the founders and original members

of the New York Stock Exchange. As trading increased, the brokers moved to 40 Wall Street.

When did the New York Stock Exchange move to its present address?

There were several more moves before the board relocated to its present address, 11 Wall Street, in 1863. That same year the board established its current name, which was the New York Stock Exchange.

When and why did the crash in the market occur?

During the 1920s, trading on the NYSE saw prices as well as volume rise. In October of 1929, Wall Street hit its worst point in history. Investors sold millions of stock shares in a very few days. Prices fell drastically and many fortunes were lost. Some investors went into debt to take advantage of the appreciating stocks. The bubble burst and the crash of 1929 brought the Dow down to the lowest point in the twentieth century. When the crash was over, the stock market spent the next ten years rebuilding and changing its systems.

NYSE

3

WALL STREET

What happened in the market between 1940 and 1960?

This was a great period for the market. It became stable, powerful and prosperous due to economic growth in the country and the public's desire to invest in securities.

What did the '70s bring as far as the market was concerned?

During this period, both the American Stock Exchange and the over-the-counter exchange became competitors with the New York Stock Exchange for company listings. During this decade, advanced computer systems changed the speed of transactions.

As a result, there was a much greater volume of trading.

What is meant by the term "the market went up or down today"?

The business of selling stocks has enjoyed a steady growth since the beginning. There were daily highs and lows.

What are the two best known numerical measures?

The best known are the Dow Jones Industrial Average (Dow) and the Standard & Poor's Stock Indexes. The S&P 500 uses a formula which takes the prices of a selected group of stocks representing different parts of the market as a whole.

WALL STREET

Where, when, and by whom was the Securities & Exchange Commission (SEC) founded?

Congress established the Securities & Exchange Commission (SEC) in 1934 to solve the problems of the Great Depression, which followed the market crash of 1929, as well as dealing with the 1920 excess boom.

When did the NYSE register as a national securities exchange?

The NYSE registered as a national securities exchange with the U.S. Securities and Exchange Commission on October 1, 1934.

Who was the primary governing body at the SEC at that time?

The Governing Committee was the primary governing body until 1938. It was at this time that the exchange hired its first paid president and created a thirty-three member Board of Governors.

Who made up the Board of Governors?

It included exchange members, out-of-town firms, non-member partners of out-of-town firms, as well as public representatives.

When was the exchange incorporated as a not-for-profit corporation?

It was incorporated in 1971. In 1972, the members voted to replace the Board of Governors with a twenty-five member board of directors comprised of a chairman and CEO, twelve representatives of the public, and twelve representatives from the securities industry.

What authority does the chairman have?

He may appoint a president, subject to the approval of the board. The president would serve as a director . . . also, at the board's discretion, they may elect an executive vice-chairman who would also serve as a director.

WALL STREET

What are the two largest stock exchanges in the world today?

The NYSE and NASDAQ.

What is the purpose of the over-the-counter (OTC) today?

The over-the-counter (OTC) is strong today because of trading regulations. It is a sophisticated telecommunications and computer network. It is ranked second in daily share volume behind the New York Stock Exchange. The OTC is another facet of the market as a whole.

What are the different departments found in the New York Stock Exchange?

The main office has trading departments for the stocks listed on different exchanges, various types of bonds, and over-the-counter stocks.

There is a research department where security analysts decide for the investor the investment potential of certain stocks and also investment strategies.

There is an underwriting department which finds buyers for new stock issues. Lastly, there is a corporate finance department which plans company financing.

When is the New York Stock Exchange open?
It is open Monday through Friday, 9:30 A.M. to 4:00 P.M. EST. It is closed on holidays.

What does the main office do?

It handles payments and safely stores stock certificates and other documents. Each investment firm must conform to SEC requirements, including additional exchange or OTC rules. These are in place to protect the investor.

WALL STREET

What must a brokerage firm have in order to do business?

All major brokerages must have membership in one or more stock exchanges. Such firms are allowed to execute orders on the exchange's trading floor.

EXCHANGE SEAT

Does owning a seat automatically give you a membership?

No, you must be reviewed by the NYSE membership department. Once admitted, you are constantly scrutinized by the NYSE and government regulators to be sure you are complying with security regulations and ethical conduct in serving your clients.

Why is a membership on the NYSE referred to as a "seat"?

In the early years, members sat in assigned chairs during the roll call of stocks. This term lost its literal meaning with the continuous trading in 1871.

What are the advantages of owning a seat?

It carries power, prestige, and responsibility. One can buy and sell securities on the floor, act as agent for others, or act for one's account.

WALL STREET

How much does a seat on the NYSE cost?

A brokerage firm must buy a seat in order to become a member. These seats are sold in their own auction market. A seat on the New York Stock Exchange in 1987 sold for one million dollars, the highest ever at that time.

How many stock exchanges are there in the United States today?

There are nine exchanges, consisting of New York Stock Exchange, American Stock Exchange, Boston Stock Exchange, Cincinnati Stock Exchange, Intermountain Stock Exchange, Midwest Stock Exchange, Pacific Stock Exchange, Philadelphia Stock Exchange, and Spokane Stock Exchange.

What two are the largest?

New York Stock Exchange and the American Stock Exchange are the two largest.

What exchanges are linked by computer system to the New York and American exchanges?

The Pacific, Midwest, Philadelphia, Boston, and Cincinnati are linked to the New York and American exchanges.

United States Stock Exchanges

● Spokane Stock Exchange

● Pacific Stock Exchange

● Intermountain Stock Exchange

● Midwest Stock Exchange

● Cincinnati Stock Exchange

Boston Stock Exchange ●

Philadelphia ● ● Stock Exchange ●

New York Stock Exchange

American Stock Exchange

WALL STREET

What must a company have before its stock can be listed?

There are certain minimum requirements a company must fill before it can be listed on the NYSE. It must have pre-tax earnings of $2.5 million in the last year, 11.1 million shares publicly held, and a minimum of 2,000 holders of 100 share lots of the stock.

Where are the Pacific exchange and Midwest exchange located?

The Pacific exchange is located in San Francisco and the Midwest exchange is located in Chicago.

Please give information about the Tokyo exchange.

The Tokyo Stock Exchange trades more shares than any other in the world. It is second only to New York in dollar value. Because Japan is so totally computerized, no stock certificates ever change hands as the computer memory holds everything.

Tell me about the London exchange.

In dollar value of trading, the London exchange is third ranked behind New York and Tokyo. It is first in the number of companies listed. The London exchange also lists bonds in addition to stocks. This accounts for their tremendous number of listings. Half of the exchange stocks are foreign.

What does the London exchange mean when they say "ordinary shares" and "gilts" or "gilt-edged" stocks?

The first term refers to common shares of stock "ordinary shares." British government bonds are referred to as "gilts" or "gilt-edged" shares.

WALL STREET

Are there other exchanges in North America?

There are major exchanges in Montreal, Toronto, and Mexico City.

What about South America?

South America has an exchange in Buenos Aires, Argentina.

Where are the major world stock exchanges located?

The major world stock exchanges are located in Mexico, Hong Kong, Australia, Singapore/Malaysia, Italy, France, London, Tokyo, and West Germany.

What is the main exchange in Canada?

The Toronto Stock Exchange is the major Canadian market. There is also the Montreal exchange and the smaller Vancouver Stock Exchange.

WORLD STOCK EXCHANGES

WALL STREET

What is the situation of stocks in China?

The newest small exchanges are in China. The Beijing exchange opened in 2003 and offered one stock only. The Shanghai exchange also opened in 2003 and was offering just four stocks and two bonds. The Beijing exchange is open only on Tuesday and Friday mornings and it has very little activity. There is daily trading in Shanghai. Unlike in other world markets, foreigners are forbidden to trade on the Chinese stock exchange.

Can a company be listed on more than one exchange in the United States?

A company can be listed on only one of the New York exchanges. In order to get a broader exposure, a company can be listed on more than one exchange in the United States.

How do you buy shares of stock?

An investor opens an account (similar to opening a bank account). Then the investor is ready to buy or sell stocks through any exchange. The individual's broker, acting as his or her agent, handles the transaction.

What does the term "market order" mean?

"Market order" refers to buying 100 shares of a stock. This is commonly called a round lot.

WALL STREET

What is meant by placing a market order and how is it done?

This order is carried out immediately at the best price available. The order is sent to the trading departments of the respective firms and directly transmitted to the NYSE's floor.

What does the "floor broker" do?
The "floor brokers" (employees located on the trading floor) receive the order. They go to the "trading post" where stock is bought and sold. The stock price is determined through supply and demand.

What is meant by regulation?

Stock watch, a computer system that looks for unusual trading patterns, contacts NYSE regulatory personnel for possible insider trading abuses or other prohibitive trading practices.

What other regulatory activities are monitored by the exchange?
Also included is the supervision of member firms to enforce compliance with operational requirements, as well as financial, periodic checks on broker's sales practices, and the constant monitoring of specialist operations.

Enforce Compliance
Monitor Sales Practices
& Special Operations

Why is the New York Stock Exchange regulated?
The regulations protect member firms and the customer, as well as the integrity of the market. The NYSE is the most active self-regulator. As billions of dollars circulate through the exchange daily, the exchange strictly enforces the regulations to be sure every transaction is handled properly.

STOCKS

STOCKS

What is meant by Dow Jones Industrial Averages?

There are 30 stocks in the index. All are excellent stocks to hold because of their reputation within each industry. They are called blue chip stocks because of their steady growth and new products. Blue chip refer to the most valuable chips in a poker game. These are the backbone of the U.S. economy. As of 2003, they include the following:

Alcoa (AA)
AT&T (T)
American Express (AXP)
Altria Group, Inc. (MO)
Boeing (BA)
Caterpillar (CAT)
Citigroup (C)
Coca-Cola (KO)
Disney (DIS)
Dupont (DD)
Eastman Kodak (EK)
Exxonmobil (XOM)
General Electric (GE)
General Motors (GM)
Hewlett-Packard Company (HWP)
Home Depot, Inc. (HD)

Honeywell (HON)
IBM (IBM)
Intel Corporation (INTC)
International Paper (IP)
Johnson & Johnson (JN)
McDonalds (MCD)
Merck (MRK)
Microsoft Corporation (MSFT)
Minnesota Mining and
Manufacturing Company (MMM)
J. P. Morgan (JPM)
Proctor & Gamble (PG)
SBC Communications (SBC)
United Technologies (UTX)
Wal-Mart (WMT)

Each stock has an abbreviation called a symbol. The above letters in parentheses are the stock symbols used to look up the stock. Symbols indicate whether the stock is on the New York Stock Exchange (3 letters or less) or the NASDAQ and American Stock Exchange (4 letters or more). Symbols with five letters ending in X are used for mutual funds.

What is an annual report?

All publicly traded companies are required by law to file annual reports describing their business and disclosing their incomes, profits, losses, and net worth.

STOCKS

What is an asset allocation?

Placing or allocating one's money or assets in a variety of places. For example, some money can be invested in stocks, bonds, and cash.

What is meant by an asset?

An individual or a company's money, investments, or property, which have value.

What does the term 'bear' refer to?

A person with a pessimistic market outlook.

What is a bear market?

A prolonged period of falling prices. It's usually brought on by declining economic activity.

What is the "big board"?

A popular term for the New York Stock Exchange.

What is a blue chip stock?

Common stock in well-known companies that have a record of profit growth, quality management, and dividend payment. There are more blue chip stocks besides those listed on Dow Industrials.

What is a bull market?

A prolonged period of rising prices in the stock market and other securities markets.

What is a call option?

The right to buy a fixed amount of a security at a designated price until the option's specified expiration date.

STOCK TRIVIA

When and Where Was the First Stock Exchange Organized?

In Philadelphia in 1790. The traders, who met every day under the buttonwood tree on Wall Street, adopted the name New York Stock Exchange.

STOCKS

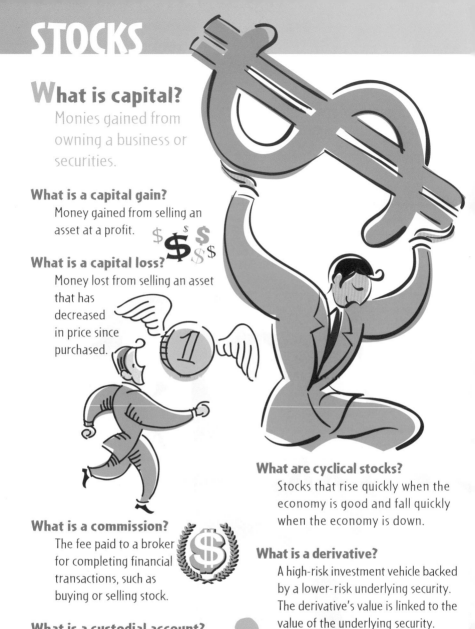

What is capital?
Monies gained from owning a business or securities.

What is a capital gain?
Money gained from selling an asset at a profit.

What is a capital loss?
Money lost from selling an asset that has decreased in price since purchased.

What is a commission?
The fee paid to a broker for completing financial transactions, such as buying or selling stock.

What is a custodial account?
An investment account opened by a friend, parent, or guardian for a minor. The parent makes investments for the child's interest until the child reaches the age of 18. Taxes are the child's responsibility.

What are cyclical stocks?
Stocks that rise quickly when the economy is good and fall quickly when the economy is down.

What is a derivative?
A high-risk investment vehicle backed by a lower-risk underlying security. The derivative's value is linked to the value of the underlying security.

STOCKS

What is a dividend?

A distribution of earnings to share-holders based on company profits. Dividends are usually paid on a per share basis every three months.

What is meant by a downgrade?

A downgrade lowers the quality rating of securities issued by a corporation or government entity.

What is Dun & Bradstreet (D&B)?

A company that combines credit information obtained from commercial firms with data solicited from their creditors and makes it available to its subscribers in reports and a rating directory.

What does earning per share (EPS) mean?

A corporation's net profits divided by the number of shares it has issued.

What is meant by fixed income?

A security that pays a fixed rate of return over a designated period of time.

What is an individual retirement account (IRA)?

A personal savings or investment account in which money is deposited and saved on a tax-deferred basis until it is withdrawn at retirement.

What is equity?

Ownership of or a stake in a company or property.

STOCKS

What is an initial public offering (IPO)?

A corporation's first offering of stock to the public.

What is insider trading?

The buying or selling of stock by someone who has knowledge, before the public does, of events that may affect the stock's price. An investor is considered an insider if he or she is part of the company's management, is on the board of directors, holds more than 10 percent of the company's shares, or has insider knowledge.

What are investments?

Use of capital to earn money through a financial instrument.

What are investment clubs?

Groups of people who pool their assets in a joint investment fund and meet regularly to share information and make joint investment decisions.

What is liquidity?

Ability to buy and sell large quantities of an asset quickly without significantly affecting the asset's price. Also, the ability to convert an asset to cash.

What does load mean?

Sales charge paid by an investor when buying shares of some mutual funds or annuities.

STOCKS

What is a margin call?

A demand that a customer, who has borrowed against securities in an account, deposit enough money to meet a minimum balance requirement after the value of the securities has dropped.

What is Moody's Investors Service?

One of the two best-known bond rating agencies in the country. It is headquartered with its parent company, Dun & Bradstreet, in downtown Manhattan. They also rate preferred and common stocks, and municipal short-term issues.

What does NASDAQ stand for?

Originally, National Association of Securities Dealers Automated Quotation. It is a computerized system that provides brokers and dealers price quotations. In 1990, the association officially changed the name to the NASDAQ Stock Market.

What is the Nikkei Stock Average?

An index of 225 leading stocks traded on the Tokyo Stock Exchange.

What is online trading?

Security transactions conducted via computer. It is another form of discount brokering. The reason for the discount is that you get no additional service other than placing the order. Online trading carries a smaller commission. The security transactions are conducted via computer. It is another form of discount brokering because you get no additional service other than placing the order. It is a tool, not a substitute for monitoring stocks.

What is an option?

Right to buy or sell a fixed amount of a security by a specific date at a specific price.

What does over-the-counter (OTC) mean?

Some securities, such as stocks and bonds, are bought or sold over the phone or computer instead of at the trading exchange. This is called over-the-counter.

STOCKS

What is par value?

Value at which a security, such as a bond, was issued or can be redeemed for cash.

What is a portfolio?

A collection of securities, such as stocks and bonds, owned by an individual or institutional investor.

What is price/earnings ratio (P/E Ratio)?

The ratio achieved by dividing a stock's price by its earnings per share. The earnings are found in the company's quarterly report or may be projected by a professional stock analyst.

What is preferred stock?

Class of capital stock that pays dividends at a specific rate and that has preference over common stock in the payment of dividends and the liquidation of assets. It does not carry voting rights.

What is a primary market?

Market for newly issued securities in which proceeds of sales go to the issuer of the securities.

What is principal?

Basic amount deposited in an account or invested in a security separate from earnings, interest, or dividends.

What is profit?

Amount earned on an investment when it is sold for more than the purchase price.

STOCKS

What is a prospectus?

Formal written offer to sell securities that provides an investor with information needed to make a decision.

What is redemption?

Repayment of a bond or preferred stock at or before the maturity date at par value or a premium.

What is meant by return?

Profit on an investment.

What is a proxy?

Someone who is authorized to speak on behalf of another, an example being one who votes on behalf of another shareholder.

What does publicly held mean?

A publicly held company is owned by those members of the public who have bought its shares of stock.

What is a rating?

It is an evaluation of a security's investment and credit risk by a rating service, such as Moody's Investors Service or Value Line Investment Survey.

STOCKS

What is a secondary market?
Bonds sold at par (face value) when issued. After issue, bonds are traded in the secondary market, which means they are bought and sold through brokers such as stocks are. The company gets no money from these secondary trades.

What are securities?
Financial instruments that represent an ownership interest in a company (stock), a creditor relationship with a corporation or government (bonds), or rights to ownership such as those represented by an option.

What is a seller's market?
A market in which demand for goods, services, or securities exceeds supply, driving up the price and increasing the seller's opportunity to sell and make a profit.

What is a share?
A unit of ownership or equity in a company or corporation.

What is a shareholder/stockholder?
An individual or institutional investor who owns shares of a company's stock.

What is a stock split?
When the price of a stock continues to rise, sometimes the board of directors of the company agrees to a stock split because the price of a share becomes too expensive for people to buy. A typical stock split is two for one, which means you will receive two shares for every one share that you own and the price for each share goes down by half. For example, if a company with stock selling at $100 per share splits the stock, a shareholder with 200 shares will now have 400 shares at a price of $50 per share.

STOCKS

What is a spread?
The difference between the bid and offer price for a security.

What is a stock?
An ownership interest in a publicly traded company, represented by a stock certificate. There are two kinds of stock; common and preferred.

*Common Stock:
Units of ownership in a public company or corporation available to all investors.

*Preferred Stock:
A class of capital stock that has preference over common stock in the payment of dividends and liquidation of assets.

SPREAD

What is Standard & Poor's Corporation?

A subsidiary of McGraw-Hill companies that provides a broad range of investment services, including rating corporate and municipal bonds, common stocks, and preferred stocks.

What is a stock index?
A statistical measure of the ups and downs of stock prices of a representative selection of stocks. For example, Standard and Poor's 500 index (S&P) measures the performance of 500 specific stocks.

23

STOCKS

What are stock markets/stock exchanges?

The physical location of the stock market is referred to as the exchange, unless the market is conducted via computer or over-the-counter.

Markets are for the sale and purchase of securities in which prices are controlled by the laws of supply and demand.

What is a stock quote?

A stock price offered to a seller or buyer based on the price at which a security is currently trading.

What is tax deferred?

Any income— earnings, interest, or dividends— that is not subject to income tax in the current tax year, but will be taxable at a future date when funds are removed from an account.

What is the trading floor?

The area of a securities exchange in which buying and selling dealers meet to trade.

What does underwrite mean?

A person assumes the risk of purchasing new issues of securities from corporations or government entities. The underwriter then sells the securities to the public in an attempt to make a profit.

What is value?

The worth of something as measured in services, goods, or a medium exchange.

STOCKS

What is valuation?
Assigning a value to an asset.

What is venture capital?
Investment money contributed to a start-up company or project by an investor, called a venture capitalist, usually in exchange for shares of the company.

Explain the difference between interest and a dividend.
When you buy a bond, you are loaning your money to the bond issuer. That entity will pay you interest on the loan. When you buy stock, the issuer will invest your money and pay a portion of its profits called a dividend.

What is volatility?
The rapid price fluctuation of a security, such as a stock.

What is volume?
The total number of shares of securities traded in a certain period of time.

What is yield?
The return on an investment. This can vary depending on when the bond is traded or if it is held till maturity.

What is the difference between a full-service broker and a discount broker?
A full-service broker can offer a great range of educated investment advice and charges a commission for his services. A discount broker offers less guidance and charges a reduced commission.

25

STOCKS

Which stock exchange has the most technology stocks and initial public offerings (IPO)?

NASDAQ

NYSE

How many companies are listed on the New York Stock Exchange?
More than 4,000.

Who was Charles Dow and when did he create the Dow Jones Industrial Average and why?

Charles Dow was born in Connecticut in 1851. In 1882, Dow and Edward Jones began to gather financial news which they published in a daily newsletter. Dow developed the first stock average that was used to gauge the progress of the entire market. Dow Jones Industrial Average was created in 1896. It was created to cut through the daily fluctuation in the market, and it is the best known of all stock market indexes.

STOCK TRIVIA

Did you know on a typical day a floor broker walks an average of 17 miles back and forth crossing the floor at the New York Stock Exchange?

When did the Great Depression begin?

The stock market crash began on Tuesday, October 29, 1929. The "crash" was a long, downward slide of the stock prices that went on for weeks, from September 3rd through November 13th, with brief upsurges after some of the worst days.

STOCKS

What are some good research sites?

Yahoo Finance:
http://quote.yahoo.com
CBS Market Research:
http://cbsmarketwatch.com
The Motley Fool: http://www.fool.com
E*Trade: http://www.etrade.com

When I buy stock in a company, what am I entitled to?

A stock certificate, which is a piece of paper, is ownership in the company. Your money is used to help the company grow and make better products to sell. This helps the company, as well as the stockholder, make more money (profit). You will receive a monthly statement and an annual report on how the stock is doing.

What determines the price of a stock?

The price of an established stock is determined by how much a buyer will pay balanced against what a seller will take.

How are stock prices priced?

Since 2001, the price appears in dollars and cents. Prior to 2001, stock prices were shown as whole numbers and fractions representing whole dollars with the fraction being converted into cents.

.0275 .032 .0875 .0675
.25

When building a portfolio, should I put all my money in one stock?

Never pick a number of stocks in the same industry. Diversify so if one industry fails, you won't lose everything. You might want pharmaceuticals, utilities, financial, or transportation. Also, investigate U.S. companies that do business outside the U.S. Look up the company's Web site to see if they do business overseas.

STOCKS

How to read a newspaper stock listing:

Stocks are listed alphabetically by exchange. Look in the stock (business) section of the paper. Find the stock listed on the correct exchange and look up the symbol.

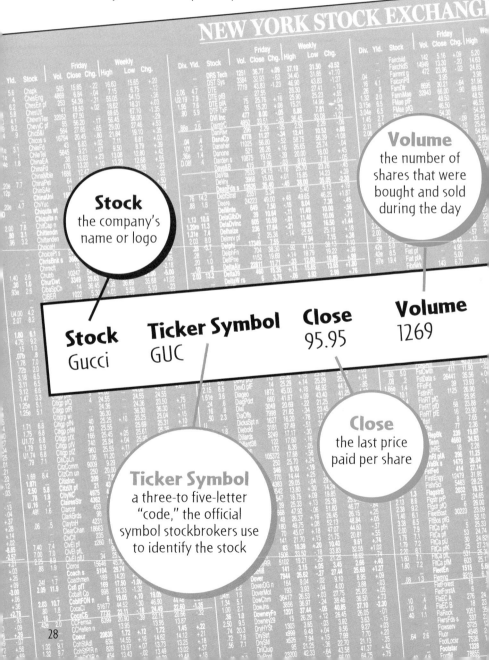

NEW YORK STOCK EXCHANGE

Volume
the number of shares that were bought and sold during the day

Stock
the company's name or logo

Stock
Gucci

Ticker Symbol
GUC

Close
95.95

Volume
1269

Close
the last price paid per share

Ticker Symbol
a three-to five-letter "code," the official symbol stockbrokers use to identify the stock

28

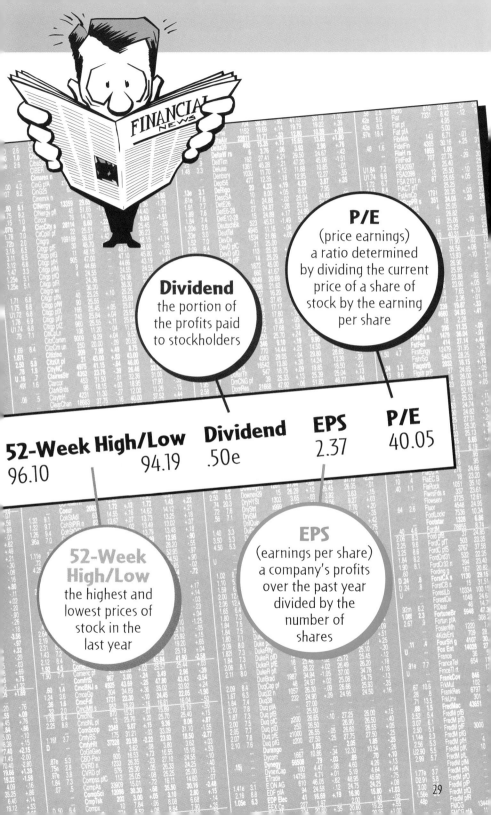

P/E
(price earnings)
a ratio determined
by dividing the current
price of a share of
stock by the earning
per share

Dividend
the portion of
the profits paid
to stockholders

52-Week High/Low   **Dividend**   **EPS**   **P/E**
96.10   94.19   .50e   2.37   40.05

**52-Week
High/Low**
the highest and
lowest prices of
stock in the
last year

EPS
(earnings per share)
a company's profits
over the past year
divided by the
number of
shares

STOCKS

What would cause a stock to fall?

Poor marketing, loss of stockholders, mergers, loss of contracts, and product recall. Most commonly, more sellers than buyers.

Are there different types of stocks?

Blue chip growth stocks are from companies with long records of earnings and dividends.

Will I always make money on my stocks?

You are never guaranteed that your stocks will go up in value. Sometimes companies don't grow or don't use their money wisely, and their stock price will drop.

What would cause a stock to rise?

- Another company buys out a company's stock

- A company's board and officers decide to buy back its stock

- A company has an increase in earnings

- A company releases new products

- The stock has more buyers than sellers

Growth stocks don't pay high dividends, but because of their steady growth are good investments and can often be sold at a profit after a few years.

PROFITS

Income stocks usually pay higher than average dividends.

STOCKS

Where are the various exchanges or associations located?

New York Stock Exchange (NYSE)
20 Broad Street
New York, NY 10005
(212) 656-3000
www.nyse.com

The National Association of Securities Dealers, Inc (NASD)
The NASDAQ Stock Market
1735 K Street, N.W.
Washington, DC 20006
(202) 496-2500
www.nas.com

The NASDAQ Stock Market (NASDAQ)
33 Whitehall Street
New York, NY 10004
(212) 858-4000
www.nasdaq.com

American Stock Exchange (AMEX)
86 Trinity Place
New York, NY 10006
(212) 306-1000
www.amex.com

When is the shareholders' meeting held?

The meeting takes place once a year, and stockholders are welcome to attend. Its purpose is to let the shareholders give input to the board

of directors on various issues pertaining to the financial health of the company. Stockholders have one vote per share at this meeting.

How do you set up a brokerage account?

The process is the same whether you use a full-service or a discount broker. You will complete an application form that gives an overview of your financial capabilities. You will be given a choice of account types. The broker will explain what the minimum deposit is and what his fee will be. Once your trade goes through, the money is due the broker in three days. If you sell stock and you are holding the stock certificate, it is due to the broker within three days of the sale. However, the broker usually holds it for you.

What are some additional online sites?

Suretrade: www.suretrade.com
Web Street Securities: www.webstreet.com
Harrisdirect: www.dljdirect.com

STOCKS

Can you list a stock market game that can be used in school?

"The Stock Market Game" (www.smgww.org) is the oldest and best-known stock market game. It began in 1977 and has been used for kids grades four through twelve. This game provides rules, a portfolio, information for teachers, and state sites which tell you how to register.

What does NAIC stand for?

This is an inexpensive plan that allows you to buy stock for a small fee in more than 160 firms. Its Web site is www.naic.org.

What should you look for when finding a broker?

Always inquire what his or her commission rate is. Also, ask if there is a maintenance fee and what the minimum balance is.

Who are some discount brokers?

Charles Schwab and Fidelity Investments commission rates are around 65% less costly than those of full-service firms. You need to do much of the homework and decision making yourself, however. They will give you a discount commission rate.

Can you buy stock on the Internet? If so, what are the names of some sellers?

If you know what you want to buy, you can contact e*trade (www.etrade.com), Ameritrade (www.ameritrade.com), or Harrisdirect (www.harris direct.com) for example. They will charge a very low commission.

Check out Gomez Advisors (www.gomez.com). They keep up with the performance of online brokers.

What are venture capitalists?

A venture capitalist is an investor who is willing to invest money in a new company he or she thinks will grow. Some firms group several of these investors together to help start a company.

STOCKS

IPO

What is meant by a company going public?

When a company goes public, it is selling stock to the public in what is called an IPO (initial public offering).

What is an advantage of having preferred stock?

Preferred stock has a fixed dividend, which means it doesn't rise or fall, regardless of whether the company increases the dividend for the common stockholders.

If a company calls its preferred stock, you must sell it back. Sometimes it may be called at a price below the market price.

What is meant by the term "points"?

This refers to how many numbers any stock market or measurement of the market went up or down (e.g. the Dow Jones Industrial Average gained 20 points).

STOCKS

What is a "day trader"? Is there a "night trader"?

A "day trader" is someone who trades in and out of stocks repeatedly, often several times a day. There is no such thing as a "night trader."

Is it better to buy stock in a new company or one that is established?

It greatly depends on your objectives and tolerance for risk. With an established company, you have a track record of stock performance to assist you.

Are companies with expensive stock a better buy?

Not necessarily, although this does represent customer confidence. Many fine corporations will split their stock, therefore doubling the number of shares already sold and enabling more investors to buy in at half the former price.

Is it true most stocks on the NASDAQ are Internet stocks?

No, the dot.com era in the 1990s created this falsehood. However, the NASDAQ does have a disproportionate number of technical stocks compared to other markets its size.

Do you have to be a college graduate to become a stockbroker? What are the requirements to become one?

No, you simply have to have a sponsor (any willing brokerage firm) and pass several tests including the Series Seven test and your own state's test.

What happens to my stock if a company I own merges with another company? How does the value of the stock change?

Merger values are determined with each individual merger agreement, so it varies greatly.

STOCKS

How does the market affect the economy?

The market provides the economy with a psychological factor. If the economy is good, the market tends to do well. In good times, investors feel more comfortable spending, thus stimulating the economy. Vice versa is also true.

Why did the market go down after 9/11?

Investors do not like uncertainty; it puts more risk into their investments. September 11 created great uncertainty in our country and stockholders sold shares.

When you sell stock, how many days does it take to get your money?

Three days.

Why do we have a stock market?

To allow individuals ownership in corporate America and the potential to prosper along with the corporation.

What should you look for in finding a stockbroker?

Call a reputable brokerage firm or ask a friend for suggestions. You should get a good feel for a broker's honesty and knowledge prior to investing with her or him.

STOCKS

Does the U.S. buy and sell the most stock?

Yes.

What is meant by the term "exchange"?

It simply refers to a "market place" where public shares are traded. Ask your broker.

What is a good growth rate for a stock?

You can look on the Internet or ask your broker how analysts are rating that stock.

Should you get a second opinion when buying stock?

It should not be necessary.

How do people forecast what will happen with a company's stock?

Analysts look at many factors to forecast a company's performance, some of which are past performance, current macroeconomic environment, management style, potential for profits, and many others.

Is there a protection program for stock buyers?

There are regulatory bodies which govern the way stockbrokers do business. The **Securities and Exchange Commission** is the main one.

SEC
Securities
& Exchange
Commission

STOCKS

Is the stock market like a business or is it run by the government?
Each exchange is run like a business; however, the Securities and Exchange Commission (SEC) is a governmental body that heavily regulates the market place.

Who runs the NYSE—one person, a board, or both? Has a woman ever headed the board?
A president and a board of governors runs the NYSE. No, there has never been a female president.

When you make money in the stock market, are you taxed, and if so, how much?
Only when you sell the stock. Your profits will be short-term gains if you hold the stock less than six months. Otherwise, they will be long-term gains. An accountant should always be advised when you are addressing your own profit picture.

Does the value of the stock depend on how many people buy it?
No, but the number of shares bought vs. sold directly influences the price of the stock. It is classic supply and demand.

Are the stock markets around the world linked together?
They are not linked together; however, there is a crossover in trading shares of certain corporations.

37

BONDS

BONDS

What are bonds?

Bonds are loans that investors make to corporations and governments. The borrowers get the cash they need while the lenders earn interest.

Is a bond safer than a stock?

Not necessarily. Each has its own risks that can vary with many factors (economic environment, health of the underlying corporation, etc.).

How is a bond's worth determined?

The value of a bond is determined by the interest it pays, allowing the borrowers to get the cash they need and lenders to earn interest.

What are municipal bonds?

These are debt obligations issued by cities, counties, and other government entities to raise money to build hospitals, sewer systems, schools, and roads.

When purchasing a municipal bond, you are lending money to an issuer who guarantees paying you a specific

rate of interest during the course of each year for a specific number of years. This money will be tax free.

What are U. S. Treasury bonds?

U. S. Treasury bonds are backed by the U.S. Government. Treasury issues are sold in $1000 increments and are available with 2-, 5-, or 10-year terms. An annual interest rate is paid on the security.

What is bond vocabulary?

The language of bonds tells potential investors the following:

FEATURE OF THE LOAN

HOW IT WILL BE REPAID

WHETHER IT'S LIKELY TO BE REPAID AHEAD OF SCHEDULE.

BOND TRIVIA

Another little-known fact is that Americans invest more in bonds than stocks or mutual funds.

BONDS

Where can investors buy and trade bonds?

Bonds can be purchased from brokers, banks, or directly from certain issuers. Activity in the bond trading room is every bit as intense as trading on the New York Stock Exchange floor.

What are junk bonds?

Junk bonds are high-risk/high-return corporate bonds that can default if the issuer fails to pay its debt.

What does book value mean?

The difference between what a company owns and what it owes.

What are mortgage-backed bonds?

Bonds that are backed by mortgage loans. They are self-amortizing, which means the payment you receive includes both the principal and interest; therefore, there is no lump sum repayment at maturity.

What are Ginnie Maes?

Bonds issued by the U.S. Government National Mortgage Association.

What is meant by a maturity date?

The date on which a bond can be redeemed by the bondholder for the full or face value.

What is "yield to maturity"?

The rate of return an investor will receive if he or she holds a long-term, interest-bearing investment, such as a bond, until its maturity date.

What is a zero coupon?

A security, such as a bond, that is sold at a deep discount of its face (or full) value and pays the holder the full appreciation at maturity instead of making periodic interest payments.

BONDS

What does it mean to buy bonds?

When buying bonds, you are loaning money to a company. Whether the company does well or not, you receive the same interest. Also, you have no say in how the company is managed.

How does the government borrow money?

The government—either national, state, county, or city—sells bonds. These bonds allow an individual to invest money for a certain length of time at a fixed interest rate. The investor will receive this interest until the bond matures. Once this happens, the principal (original investment) will be returned to you.

Is a fixed interest rate a good thing?

It depends. Should the interest rate on your bonds change and the interest rates on new bonds are lower, your bond becomes more valuable. If the interest rate on new bonds is higher, your bond becomes less valuable.

What are Freddie Macs?

Bonds issued by the Federal Home Loan Mortgage Corporation (FHLMC).

What are Fannie Maes?

Bonds issued by the Federal National Mortgage Association (FNMA).

What are some popular types of bonds?

Corporate Bonds: ✔

Corporate bonds usually are rated from AAA to C. Investors buy them to increase their chances for a higher level of income. They pay interest semiannually.

Junk Bonds:

Junk bonds are the lowest-rated corporate and municipal bonds. They are a poor-quality investment and may default in the future. They are not insured by the U.S. Government.

Municipal Bonds: ✔

Used by townships, cities, or counties to raise money to pay for projects such as highways, bridges, and schools.

Long Bonds:

Another name is 30-year treasury bonds. They're issued by the U. S. Treasury Department to fund various government activities and to help pay off the national debt.

BONDS

What is Moody's Investors Service?
One of the two best-known bond rating agencies in the United States. It is headquartered at its parent company, Dun & Bradstreet, in downtown Manhattan. Moody's rates preferred and common stocks and municipal short-term issues. Moody's also rates most publicly held corporate and municipal bonds and treasury and government agency issues.

What is par value?
The value at which a security, such as a bond, was issued or can be redeemed for cash.

What is a rating?
The evaluation of a security's investment and credit risk by a rating service, such as Moody's Investors Service or Value Line Investment Survey.

What is redemption?
It is the repayment of a bond or preferred stock at or before the maturity date, at par value or at a premium.

What is required to hold a bond?
A bond can be kept until its maturity date (the date at which the borrower has to pay the money back) or one can also sell the bond before it matures to another investor.

When do bond prices change?
They change in price when interest rates change. They go down when the interest rate goes up; they go up when the interest rate goes down.

What is a bond's credit rating?
A credit rating rates the borrower's ability to pay back the loan. If the company is able to pay the loan, it will have an AAA credit rating. C's and D's are the worst ratings. Bondholders are usually paid before stockholders, should the company go bankrupt.

How can you find out the interest rate a federal government bond is paying?
The U.S. Treasury Web site is www.savingsbonds.gov.

MUTUAL FUNDS

MUTUAL FUNDS

What is a mutual fund?

A fund of many different companies' securities (stocks and bonds) held together under one name, allowing an investor to buy into the fund and thereby own many different companies for one purchase. The following are types of mutual funds.

$ **Growth funds:** ✔
Investments in securities likely to increase in value in the future.

$ **Money market funds:**
Investments in certificates of deposit. This offers check writing privileges and can be converted to cash.

$ **No-load funds:** ✔
The fund company sells these directly to the investor with no sales charge.

$ **Global funds:**
Investments in securities of companies or governments in the U.S. and throughout the world.

$ **Income funds:** ✔
Investment in securities paying a regular income to the investor through dividends or interest.

$ **International funds:**
Investment in securities of companies or governments throughout the world, excluding the United States.

MUTUAL FUNDS

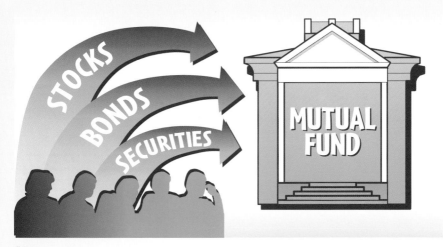

How is a mutual fund put together?

An investment company buys the stock and/or bonds of numerous companies of a certain type and pools them together into one fund name to offer to the public.

What was the first mutual fund and when was it created?

Massachusetts Investors Trust, which was created in 1924, was the first mutual fund. Its purpose was to act as a private firm for its own investors. It's still in business and operating seven funds that are open to all investors.

What is the objective of a mutual fund?

Every mutual fund, stock, bond, or money market is established with a specific investment objective that fits into one of three basic goals:

- $ Current income
- $ Future growth
- $ Both income and growth

MUTUAL FUNDS

What is net asset value?

Current market value of a share of a mutual fund.

What is the largest mutual fund in the country?

Fidelity Magellan Fund is one of the largest and has over $100 billion in assets. It is a growth fund that invests in the stocks that will increase in price rather than in stocks that pay dividends.

Do mutual funds pay dividends like stock?

They do pay dividends, and they can be either taken in cash or be automatically reinvested in the fund.

What is the minimum it takes to invest in a mutual fund?

This can vary depending on the fund. You need to check on different funds. Some funds have automatic monthly investment programs. With this type of program, you can arrange to have as little as $20 a month wired out of your checking account directly to the fund.

Who watches the fund?

The fund provides professional management. A portfolio manager is responsible for choosing which stocks or bonds are in the fund.

What is the advantage of being in a mutual fund?

In the event individual stocks in the fund go down, you won't notice the downturn as much because you are holding many companies with the fund.

Is there a fee to buy into a fund?

There is an administrative fee which pays the manager who is handling the fund. This is referred to as an expense ratio, and the charge is usually a percentage of your investment.

MUTUAL FUNDS

How many mutual funds are out there?

There are over 10,000 mutual funds in the United States today, the value of which is around $7 trillion. In 2003, they had approximately 83 million investors.

What is the difference between load and no-load funds?

Load funds, sold by brokers, receive a percentage of the individual's investment and the fee is usually 2 percent, 3 percent, or 5 percent. This fee is deducted when you buy the fund. 2% 3% 5%

No-load funds have no fee to buy a fund but there is a charge to sell the shares. This is figured on a sliding scale. The longer you own the fund the lower it goes. You also pay an annual fee.

Isn't it better to buy the no-load fund?

That depends on what you are buying. It's true you will save a fee by buying the fund directly from the issuing company.

What is net asset value? (NAV)

It is the price of one share of a mutual fund. Just look for your fund in the newspaper or online and check for the NAV.

What is NET CHG?

This stands for net change, which shows the up or down change in price since yesterday.

What is YTD percent RET?

This stands for year-to-date percentage return or how much the fund has been up or down since the first of the year.

MUTUAL FUNDS

How to read a newspaper mutual fund quotation:
Mutual funds are listed alphabetically by exchange. Look in the mutual funds report (business) section of the paper.

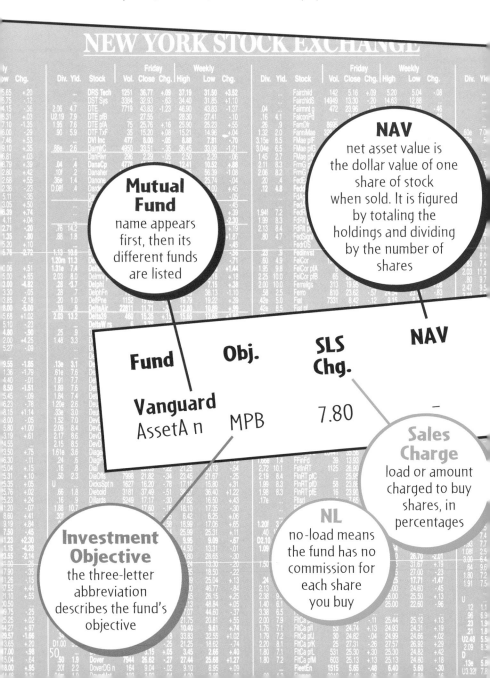

NEW YORK STOCK EXCHANGE

Mutual Fund
name appears first, then its different funds are listed

NAV
net asset value is the dollar value of one share of stock when sold. It is figured by totaling the holdings and dividing by the number of shares

Fund	Obj.	SLS Chg.	NAV
Vanguard AssetA n	MPB	7.80	—

Sales Charge
load or amount charged to buy shares, in percentages

NL
no-load means the fund has no commission for each share you buy

Investment Objective
the three-letter abbreviation describes the fund's objective

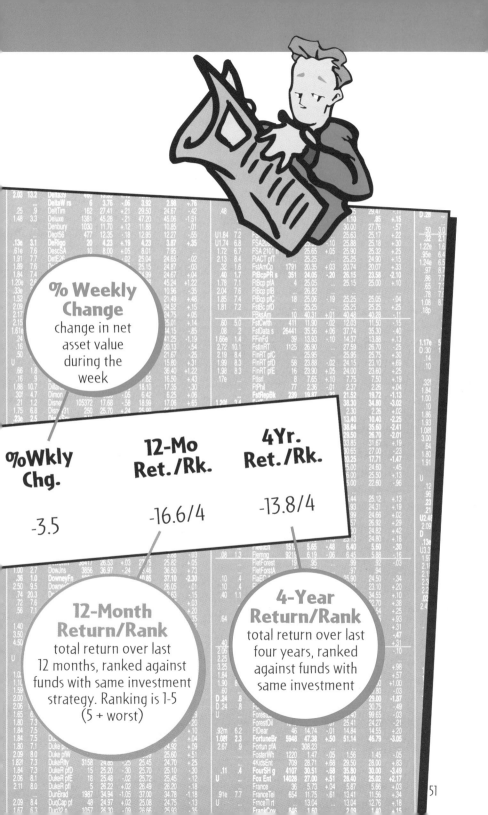

% Weekly Change change in net asset value during the week

%Wkly Chg.
-3.5

12-Mo Ret./Rk.
-16.6/4

4Yr. Ret./Rk.
-13.8/4

12-Month Return/Rank total return over last 12 months, ranked against funds with same investment strategy. Ranking is 1-5 (5 + worst)

4-Year Return/Rank total return over last four years, ranked against funds with same investment

51

MUTUAL FUNDS

Do you pay tax when you sell your mutual fund?

Yes, you do, if you have made a profit.

Why are mutual funds so popular?

Mutual funds are popular because of their liquidity and because they offer diversification. A mutual fund has low operating costs, continuous management, and shareholder services, such as automatic reinvestment of dividends and/or interest.

What is Morningstar?

Morningstar is a well-known rating company that offers news stories and analyses on the world of funds. It carries its mutual fund expertise to the Web. (www.morningstar.com).

Why is the Vanguard 500 Index Fund important and when did it start?

Vanguard (under a different name) was founded by John C. Bogle and was the first retail index fund. In 2000, it became the largest mutual fund holding company ever with $100 billion in assets.

Can mutual funds be used in an IRA account?

Yes, the IRA provisions made in 1981 allowed investors to contribute $2000 a year. They are very popular in 401(K)s, IRAs, and Roth IRAs.

TICKER
TRIVIA

TICKER TRIVIA

Did you know the trading day begins at 9:30 A.M. EST/EDT and ends at 4:00 P.M. when the bell is rung at the podium?

Did you know the trading floor is where buy and sell orders are executed? People wear different colored jackets indicating their different jobs:

> Blue: messengers
> Navy: reporters
> Green: floor supervisors

Do you know who invented the electronic moving stock ticker? Thomas Edison in 1870.

10 PERCENT A YEAR

Did you know stocks have increased in price an average of 10 percent a year since 1926?

AMSTERDAM

Did you know the Nikkei Stock Average is an index of 225 stocks trading on the Tokyo Stock Exchange? The symbol for the Tokyo Stock Exchange is (TSE).

Did you know the first stock exchange began in Amsterdam, Holland, in 1602 where shares of the United East India Company were traded?

TICKER TRIVIA

Did you know there are over 10,000 mutual funds in the United states?

Bet you didn't know the New York Stock Exchange's first home was a second-story room located at 40 Wall Street. The rent was $200 per year in 1817.

Bet you didn't know there are currently 1,366 seats on the NYSE! Did you know owners of stock market seats may lease their seats?

EXCHANGE SEAT

Bet you didn't know the bell, rung daily, is part of the NYSE's heritage and that it is considered an honor to be invited to ring the opening and closing bell.

Did you know there are more than 51 million Americans who own stock?

Do you know that a penny stock is a stock not listed on one of the major exchanges and is one that sells for $5.00 or less?

Did you know in 1996 the NYSE became the first stock exchange to adopt hand-held wireless telephones for trading?

NYSE

TICKER TRIVIA

Did you know the giant bell, measuring 18" in diameter, is on a platform above the trading floor?

Did you know there are 20 trading posts located on the floor of the NYSE?

Did you know the trading posts are manned by a specialist and specialist clerks?

Bet you didn't know the trading floor is 36,000 square feet!

Did you know that every listed security is traded at one of the posts by a specialist and that this is where all the buying and selling takes place?

Did you know the computer monitor above each trading post lists data about each stock and that it shows its last price and whether it went up or down from the previous price?

Did you know the anatomy of a trade means an investor places an order to buy or sell company shares listed on the NYSE?

TICKER TRIVIA

Did you know the trading floor is where all NYSE transactions take place? Also, this is where specialists represent the orders of buyers and sellers to determine prices.

Did you know there are 1,500 trading booths where brokers obtain orders? They're transmitted to broker booth locations by telephone or electronically. Various stocks are traded at these posts. In order to keep track accurately, each company's stock trades at only one post.

INDEX

INDEX

INDEX

About the Author

Over the years, Susie Vaccaro Hardeman has been associated
with three major brokerage firms–Merrill Lynch, Dean Witter,
and E. F. Hutton–doing everything from charting commodities
and stocks to writing and entering buy and sell orders,
research, and organizing seminars. She lives in Little Rock,
Arkansas.